Sex from a man's prespective

Sex from a man's prespective

CONTENTS

I dedicate this book to my wife, Yolanda F. Alexander

A thriving marriage requires consistent sexual intimacy, not just as a physical act but as a spiritual and emotional connection that strengthens the bond between husband and wife.

Imagine a man who leaves his home each day surrounded by temptation. Billboards, commercials, and even coworkers unintentionally invite his attention.

Now, imagine this man comes home to a spouse who has neglected one of his deepest needs — intimacy. Over time, frustration sets in, resentment builds, and what once was a safe and passionate relationship turns cold. This isn't just speculation — it's a silent epidemic destroying marriages from the inside out.

Sexual intimacy is not optional in a healthy marriage. It is essential. The Bible itself teaches, "Defraud ye not one the other... that Satan tempt you not"
(1 Corinthians 7:5). This is not a mere suggestion — it is a divine warning. When a wife meets her husband's sexual needs regularly, she does more than offer physical satisfaction — she communicates love, respect, and emotional presence. These are not superficial pleasures but core to a man's sense of identity and connection.

Opponents argue that sex should not be a duty or expectation. But this is a misunderstanding. Intimacy in marriage is not about obligation — it's about partnership. Just as a husband is expected to protect, provide, and cherish, a wife is called to nurture, respect, and connect. It's a mutual exchange that fosters security and joy.

The feminist movement has done much good, but in its efforts to elevate women's independence, it has sometimes undermined the beauty of interdependence within marriage. By making men feel wrong for their natural desires, we've damaged the very fabric of what makes marriage work. If we want faithful men, we must cultivate faithful, connected relationships. And that means prioritizing sex, not occasionally, but intentionally, consistently, and with joy.

A wise woman will see intimacy not as a chore, but as a tool, to protect her marriage, affirm her husband, and fulfill her God-given role. You don't need to look far to see the cost of withholding this gift: broken homes, wandering hearts, and unspoken pain. However, the good news is that healing begins with one choice: to reconnect.

The history of Man

Over the years, men have lost their traditional role and have become something else. They do not know
what a man should be like or what a man's role is supposed to be.

Before we get into the subject " Sex from a man's Perspective", I would like to go back and set the
foundation of a man.

Adam and Eve
Image from Artlist.IO

From the beginning, God created man to be the foundation of the family. That is the reason God made man before He created the woman.

Just as in creation, God created everything in the earth that would support mankind. He provided all that mankind would need to survive on the planet. Then God created man, but He did not make a mate for man until later. Man needed to realize that something was missing from his life. All the animals that Adam named had their counterpart.

Each male animal had a female, but the man did not have someone to complete him, a person that he could connect with on his level. Someone to fulfill his needs completely because animals could not fulfill man's need for intimacy on the mental, spiritual, emotional, or physical level. Man needed someone like him.

So God decided to fulfill this need in man and provide him a helper to help him accomplish the mandate given by God.

And God blessed them, and God said unto them, Be fruitful, and multiply, and replenish the earth, and subdue it: and have dominion over the fish of the sea, and over the fowl of the air, and over every living thing that moveth upon the earth. Genesis 1:28

Man could not do this alone. So God created him a woman to fulfill all his needs. The companionship that man could not find in the animal kingdom. Eve was made perfectly to satisfy everything that Adam needed. Adam would love this woman, provide for, protect, and be the object of her desire.

Sex defines a Man

As I established, a man will go out of his way to take care of his family when he is in love with his wife. This is a given because it is in his DNA to work, provide, and protect things that belong to him. If there is no commitment, he will not give himself to a person.

Men have some needs; however, sex is at the top of their list. It's not all-consuming, but it is at the front of his mind. This is a gift from God. For so long, women have been complaining because a man approaches them to try to establish a relationship. This might not be love at first, but it can grow into something more. The main drive for a man is a sexual connection. It is a powerful force or desire that drives a man to be aggressive and to win the affections of the one he is pursuing.

Without this desire, a man would be like a woman. Today, when a man starts taking sex change drugs, it takes away the man's natural sex drive, which makes him a neutered person.

Over the years, the feminist movement has achieved the goal of transforming men into something that resembles a more feminine version of masculinity.
One that have feelings like a woman but is in a male frame.

3

Women are built for the job

There is one paramount need of a man in a marriage relationship, and that is sexual fulfillment from his wife.

The man married his wife so that this need would be fulfilled, and he does not need to pursue other women to get the satisfaction; his wife should be given to him.

However, this seems to be the hardest thing for a wife to do. Your husband appreciates your respect, your attentiveness, your care, a clean house, and food on the table. However, this is easy because it does not take a lot of sacrifice. Fulfilling your husband's sexual needs takes effort and sacrifice of your time. Often, this area lacks in many marriages and can be remedied by being aware of the importance and the makeup of a man.

Usually, women your mind is filled with other things to accomplish, but not with your husband's needs. You have to make your husband a priority.

Keeping your husband's sacks (testicles) empty daily is what will keep your marriage affairproof. There will be less temptation for him in the world because he is getting what he needs from his wife, rather than from the woman at his workplace.

When you are intimate with your husband, he receives affirmation from you and knows that he is desired and that his sexual well-being is important to you. This will protect him from outside enticement of other women.

Sex with your husband should be a daily connection. However, there are times you can not have intercourse with your husband; there are other ways to meet his needs through manual or oral stimulation to ensure that your husband's sacks are empty before he leaves the house or when he comes home from work.

> Defraud ye not one the other, except it be
> with consent for a time, that ye may give
> yourselves to fasting and prayer; and come
> together again, that Satan tempt you not for
> your incontinency. 1 Corinthians 7:5

God has instructed the married couple to come together and connect intimately daily, so the Devil will not have grounds to tempt.

There should never be a "no to sex" for either the husband or wife, but they should be willing to meet the needs of their partner.

This is the most significant area Satan will tempt a couple because one or the other's needs are not being met sexually.

For a man just leaving the house, there is a cornucopia of visual temptations. There are women who are looking for attention; they are out there
advertising their goodies. This is a battle when a man is not sexually satisfied by his wife. You have to remember that the enemy is always
looking for a way to break up a marriage. And there are many volunteers out there who would love to sleep with your husband.

4

Sex is a life giver

Many needs are fulfilled in the act of sex with your husband; it refreshes the love and respect for each other.

When this sex is lacking, the enemy has the right to attack. God created a husband and wife to connect; this is why he states that you should come together as much as possible, and the only reason He said to refrain is during a time of fasting and prayer. However, because of the lack of obedience to God's Word, the enemy has entered many marriages and destroyed them. Visit the county office in the family court system, and you will see people lined up to file for divorce. This is due to the hardness of their heart, as well as unforgiveness. Simply because they have not been taught what God requires in marriage, the devil has taken advantage of the lack of knowledge of God's Word..

A man will become drawn away to another lover because he is frustrated, unhappy, and depressed sexually unfulfilled. Irritated because he is lacking his most basic need, sexual intimacy with his wife. Most of the time, a man will not express this emotion to his wife. He does not want to be seen as needy. So, he will start looking at pron, engaging in conversations with other women, and seeking something that will fill this void. For a man, his sexual desire is basically out of his control because God has placed in him the desire to connect with someone sexually. Hence the wife. The wife is his life giver; she can meet all his needs and allow him to express himself freely.

What a gift you are to your husbands. Proverbs 31:28-28
[28] Her children arise up, and call her blessed; her husband also, and he praiseth her.
[29] Many daughters have done virtuously, but thou excellest them all.

Proverbs 31 and 11 also say, 11 The heart of her husband doth safely trust in her, so that he shall have no need of spoil. Your husband solely relies on you for his sexual health, and he trusts you with this and no other. Sex is a wonderful thing God created. Humans are different from all other animals. We can have sex with our partner face to face and not like animals. We can look into each other's eyes and experience what the other is feeling by looking at them. No other creature on this earth can do the same. What a great God we serve.

Why God created women

Neither was the man created for the woman, but the woman for the man. **1 Corinthians 11:9**

God created the woman to meet the man's needs, both intimately and domestically. When God created man, God gave him a sexual
craving for pleasure from his wife. God did not provide this desire for any other creature.

The wife's duty is to meet her husband's sexual needs. However, this seems to have gone by the wayside. Today, this has become skewed by the
feminist movement, which said that all focus should be placed on the woman to fulfill her emotional needs. Satisfying your husband's sexual need should not be grudging, but with a willingness to see him happy and satisfied.

The man is a part of your (one flesh). Most people will do everything possible to keep themselves satisfied and happy. Because you are mar-ried, your spouse in apart of your flesh. The reason for marriage (for women) is to find someone that will protect you, care for you, love you, comfort you, to give you a sense of belonging, to have a father for your children, and friendship.

The reason for marriage for men is companionship, some one to care for and sexual fulfillment.

God created woman to fulfill the needs of the man in all ways. The problem is the enemy has got women to believe that man was made for them.

There are many book written about how a man should feel the woman's emotional need and that the man should "feel" like the woman do.

The whole concept is from the devil, trying to feminize the man to be like the woman. God has created these differences between man and woman

so that they can compliment each other.

However today you see more and more men putting on heels and dresses and losing their masculinity and making a shortage of men to marry.

Sex is a top priority for men

Allow your husband time for personal communication. In the area of sex, a man feels:

Loved
Satisfied
Empowered
Relaxed
Encouraged
Desired
Wanted
Respected

The wife needs to be desirous of her husband, emotionally present, active, and willing to please. Even at times, initiating the sex and being willing to be creative, keeping sex exciting.

A man knows when his wife is not into sex. This is a turn-off for most men; they derive some of their pleasure from their wives' reactions to them.

Sleep sex, lazy sex, communicate that you are not present, and his feelings do not matter. In this intimate setting, the wife's needs are met.

Intimacy with your husband enables personal, heartfelt communication during your cuddling time. Affection is also achieved when you are dressed softly by your sweet husband. You also receive emotional close-ness and support during this time, along with acceptance of who you are. Your husband desires you totally and appreciates you just the way you are. This time of intimacy allows both of you to grow closer to-gether leaving no room for outside intrusions by the enmey.

Intimacy

Adam and Eve Together
Image from Artlist.io

What a beautiful scene

A bundle of myrrh is my well-beloved unto me; he

shall lie all night betwixt my breasts. **Song of Solomon 1:13**

Intimacy allows both to slow down and focus on the needs of each other. To push out all outside distractions so each can build up the other emotionally and spiritually. This is why God said that a man should leave his mother and father and cleave unto his wife and become one flesh (have sex).

The benefits of sexual intimacy

The wife gets to carry her husband's seed (sperm). Because sperm has benefits for the wife. It has been found that exposure to her husband's semen is good for the wife's health because of the mood-altering chemicals in his sperm. It elevates mood, increases affection, and induces sleep, while also containing vitamins and anti-depressants. Allhealth.com Benefits of sperm in the female body; Dr. Sharon Kumar, 2025

A study from the State University of New York found that women who had unprotected sex (without a condom) and were exposed to semen reported feeling less depressed. The more often and more recently they were exposed to semen, the better their mood seemed to be".

God was so mindful when he created sex to ensure the couples would grow closer and together each time they were intimate.

The importance of sexual intimacy

It fosters a sense of connection, security, togetherness, and well-being, as well as a feeling of being seen and supported. Sex is a healthy plan for the husband and wife. The more you do it, the more beneficial it is for both of you.

Scriptures

So God created man in his own image, in the image of God created he him; male and female created he them. And God blessed them, and God said unto them, Be fruitful, and multiply, and replenish the earth, and subdue it: and have dominion over the fish of the sea, and over the fowl of the air, and over every living thing that moveth upon the earth. **Genesis 1:27-28**

And the Lord God said, It is not good that the man should be alone; I will make him an help meet for him. **Genesis 2:18**

And the Lord God caused a deep sleep to fall upon Adam, and he slept: and he took one of his ribs, and closed up the flesh instead thereof;

And the rib, which the Lord God had taken from man, made he a woman, and brought her unto the man. And Adam said, This is now bone of my bones, and flesh of my flesh: she shall be called Woman, because she was taken out of Man. Therefore shall a man leave his father and his mother, and shall cleave unto his wife: and they shall be one flesh. And they were both naked, the man and his wife, and were not ashamed. **Genesis 2:21-25**

God created the woman to be all that man needs, and she was perfect, a perfect package. God has given you the looks, the body, the softness, and the sweet voice that would captivate a man for a lifetime.

Ladies, you were created to satisfy your husbands' every need. God has made you complete to fulfill the passions of your husband.

> And Jacob loved Rachel; and said, I will serve thee seven years for Rachel **Genesis 20:18**

From the beginning, marriage was intended to be the vehicle for achieving a life of love and intimacy with one's partner. Marriage is not obsolete, and the benefits outweigh a life of singleness. Not saying being single is bad. And I know that some people are called to singleness, either by their own will or by force, for physical reasons.

Proposal
Image from Artist.io

The Lie

Couple Together
Image from Artlist.io

The devil has lied to you, ladies. He has told you that you are not precious and perfectly made. You were created to fulfill a purpose. From the beginning, you were designed to be your husband's helper. To submit to your husband's leadership and help him to accomplish his God given purpose.

The devil has told you that you do not need a man (husband). That you can do it all by yourself. This is the reason there are so many women having children out of wedlock. The devil has convinced you that being a baby mama is the thing to be. Look around and you can see that this is not God's best for you.

In the beginning, God established marriage to meet all your needs, and it remains His plan today. God created sex so that you would get married.

The devil has polluted your minds and values, and you have fallen into his trap. You are going about giving away all your precious

goods to anyone who says they love you. Truly, if that person loved you, he would not have sex with you until he had asked for your hand in marriage.

Now that is LOVE!

> Marriage is honourable in all, and the bed
> undefiled: but whoremongers and
> adulterers God will judge.
>
> **Hebrews 13:4**

God's purpose for you is to save yourself until the day you are married and say "I DO" and sign the papers. This is God's best for you.

Don't believe the lie of the devil. Your purpose is to be a wife, love your husband, and love your children.

Aman.

10

Grocery Store

To ensure that your marriage is affairproof, you need to be your husband's "Grocery Store". A grocery store owner tries to have items that will

keep you in their store so you will not go to another place to find the items you are looking for. This is why most stores will ask if you can't find an item, let you know and retrieve it for you. These stores want to provide everything you want and need to keep you coming back to their store.

You need to be the grocery store for your husband, providing all that he needs and wants. You want him to keep shopping in your store because you have the best products stocked. You want your husband not to have to leave your store to find what he needs at another store.

I am a wall, and my breasts like towers: then was I
in his eyes as one that found favour.
Song of Solomon 8:10

Let her be as the loving hind and pleasant roe; let her breasts satisfy
thee at all times;
and be thou ravished always with her love. **Proverbs 5:19**

Thou hast ravished my heart, my sister, my spouse; thou hast ravished
my heart with one of thine

eyes, with one chain of thy neck.
Song of Solomon 4:9

You must realize that God has equipped you with all your husband needs until the day he dies. What a wonderful gift God has given you. Many women discount themselves because of something they dislike about themselves. They see themself as something other than beautiful and equipped to minister to their husband. If you could see yourself from your husband's eyes, your perception of yourself would change. You are desired above all other women in the world because he has chosen to walk by your side and share intimate moments with him. Again what a wonderful gift you are to your husband.

Adam and Eve Together
Image from Artlist.io

Family
Image from Artlist.io

11

Man is a gift

God created the man to be a blessing to his wife and family. God made him to be strong and to handle tough things.

God has given man the ability to think ahead and prepare for future ups and downs, as well as given him the instinct to protect those he loves with his life if it comes down to it. His innate desire is to ensure that his family is well provided for and that there will be no lack.

He is the foundation upon which the whole family stands. He is the one God talks to, to give him guidance to lead his family. He is the one who carries the seed to reproduce children.

He is the fiber that holds the family together.

Today, men are often discounted and portrayed as weak and unable to handle or provide for their families. Many men of this generation have not been taught how to be a family man. In contrast, this was not the case in the past. There are fewer and fewer examples of married men. Today, you see men having children out of wedlock, living together, not being married. This is a travesty, and women are helping this to occur by not insisting that the man wait for sex until marriage.

Without God in a man's life, this will continue to happen. A man is a gift given by God to hold society together through the confines of marriage. This is the reason God created man first. To be a benefit to his wife and his children. the intimacy with his wife is the glue that will keep them together. Just as the foundation of a house holds up the wall and ceiling, so is the man to his family.

12

Prayer

If you are struggling in the area of sex with your husband for whatever reason. It is God's will for you to connect as much as possible so the devil won't get a foothold in your marriage.

Here is a prayer to help you:

Do nothing out of selfish ambition or vain conceit. Rather, in humility value others above yourselves, not looking to your own interests but each of you to the interests of the others.
Philippians 2:2,4 NIV

Wife
Image from Artlist.io

Father, forgive me for being selfish and not following your instructions concerning my relationship with my husband. Father, help me to be more attentive to my husband's needs. I understand that our intimacy helps to keep my husband saved and keeps the tempter at bay. Thank you, Lord, for leading me to this material and reaffermining me that I am enough and was created to uplift my husband sexually.

Thank you, Lord, for your plan for my life is perfect, and I thank you.

In Jesus' name.

God's plan was perfect from the beginning. However, the devil has been working since Adam and Eve to destroy God's best for your marriage.

Kick the devil out of your marriage today and become more connected intimately with your husband as God intended.

A final word

The Bible is full of scriptures about husbands and wives. How they are supposed to treat each other, how they are to encourage one another, as well as live together in peace. Marriage is supposed to reflect Jesus and the church to the world. Marriage represents God's kingdom and the family of God. Marriage is the gospel shown to all people. It is the institute set up by God, and all people need to read the instructions to have a happy and fulfilling marriage. Simply a way to treat one another with respect and love.

God has given us a way to have heaven here on earth. And the four and twenty elders and the four beasts fell down and worshipped God that sat on the throne, saying, Amen; Alleluia. And a voice came out of the throne, saying, Praise our God, all ye his servants, and ye that fear him, both small and great. And I heard as it were the voice of a great multitude, and as the voice of many waters, and as the voice of mighty thunderings, saying, Alleluia: for the Lord God omnipotent reigneth. Let us be glad and rejoice, and give honour to him: for the marriage of the Lamb is come, and his wife hath made herself ready. And to her was granted that she should be arrayed in fine linen, clean and white: for the fine linen is the righteousness of saints
Revelation 19: 4-8
Thank You, Jesus

Pastor A. D. Alexander has been a Christian for thirty-five years. He is the father of five children and has been married to his wife, Yolanda, for eleven years. Pastor Alexander and Yolanda have nine grandchildren. Pastor Alexander was called to minister and pastored a church for twenty years.

www.ingramcontent.com/pod-product-compliance
Lightning Source LLC
Chambersburg PA
CBHW071547120626
46550CB00006B/2608